◁ **W9-CAU-526**

Keep yourself *stirred* up!

KCM Partners are invited to visit:

BELIEVERS' ACADEMY

····KCM.ORG/STIRYOURSELFUP····

for a **FREE** 10-video teaching series on how to *Stop Spiritual Drought.*

Stir up the gift of God, which is in thee by the putting on of my hands. For God hath not given us the spirit of fear; but of power, and of love, and of a sound mind. Be not thou therefore ashamed of the testimony of our Lord, nor of me his prisoner: but be thou partaker of the afflictions of the gospel according to the power of God.

2 Timothy 1:6-8

Table of Contents

Introduction

In West Texas we have a small gourd that looks much like a melon or a squash, but contains no edible fruit. It's the emptiest, hollowest, driest thing you can imagine. It grows and dies in the hot Texas sun, and is of no use to anyone except as an ornament or when hollowed out for use as a utensil. Some people use them for dipping water.

Years ago, I let myself get into a place spiritually where I was just as dry and empty as one of those gourds. It happened during one of the greatest steps of faith and expansion of outreach Kenneth Copeland Ministries has ever taken. At a time when I should have been a wellspring of life and faith, I felt more like that hollowed-out water dipper. I knew Jesus' promise that "he that believeth on me, as the scripture hath said, out of his belly shall flow rivers of living water" (John 7:38). But at that particular moment, I couldn't even find the creek bank, much less the river!

I wasn't running from God. I wasn't afraid of the impossible. I'd been in the walk of faith long enough that I thrived on God's Anointing and outpouring. I was actually looking forward to the enjoyment of seeing Him come through on this giant step of faith for our ministry. But it seemed at times, I would never make it. I kept looking for God to stir me up, but nothing seemed to be happening.

Any believer can find himself in that same place. It may be that you're a new believer who has seen the power of God work dramatically in your salvation and deliverance. Or, you may be an experienced believer, mature in The WORD, who has just committed yourself to the greatest step of obedience and faith you've ever taken. You know every step of this new life is by faith. You know this faith venture is only possible because of God's faithfulness. There's no doubt where the source of your life and victory is, yet you find yourself empty.

What you need is to stir *yourself* up—and stay stirred up in God. Especially in these last days, you need to know all that God has put in you—and how to reach down into your spirit deeper than you've ever reached before.

The truths you are about to read helped pull me out of my time of dryness and spiritual drought. They'll not only help you stir yourself up, but show you, from this time forward, how to keep yourself stirred up all the time. As you read, keep your heart and mind open, and let them be flooded with life and the lifestyle of Jesus— the lifestyle of faith, love, joy, peace and victory. Learn what God has already deposited within you and how to reach down inside your spirit to activate the gift of His life and Anointing in you...*Stir Yourself Up!*

—*Kenneth Copeland*

1

CHAPTER

YOU CAN'T
RUN
ON EMPTY!

YOU CAN'T RUN ON EMPTY!

In 1988, God gave Gloria and me some direction we didn't really want to hear. It came during a time of pressure for us. The finances of the ministry were down. Physically and emotionally, I was lower than I'd been in years. Right in the middle of that difficult time, God gave us a command. He said we were to go on television—daily.

I felt overwhelmed. *Surely this couldn't be from God*, I thought. Stock in television preachers was at an all-time low. I wanted to get *off* television, not double my TV budget!

But the more I prayed, the bigger that command from God grew. It was like chewing a piece of rawhide. It wouldn't go away. The more I said no, the bigger His *yes* became inside me. Finally, I admitted that no matter how I felt about it, that was what The LORD had instructed me to do, and I would do it.

Thankfully, I'd learned years before not to depend on feelings or circumstances in my walk with God. So I said, "God, You're calling me into something that's impossible. I have sense enough to see the only way to do this is by faith. Now I know I have faith. But if You don't stir me up, LORD, I don't know what I'll do because I don't have enough spiritual energy to reach this goal."

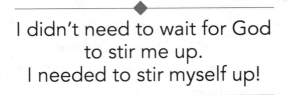

I didn't need to wait for God
to stir me up.
I needed to stir myself up!

I waited, expecting The LORD to stir me up.

I soon realized what I needed to do was stir up what God had already put within me. I needed to see that He had already given me everything I needed, to do what He had called me to do. It was there inside me because Jesus Christ, the Anointed One and His Anointing, was in me, and He had given me His Anointing. I didn't need to wait for God to stir me up. I needed to stir myself up!

Apparently I wasn't the first minister to face that problem. In the early days of the Church, a discouraged young minister named Timothy needed to know that. The good news was that God was aware of Timothy's need, and there was a man in the Body of Christ with God's heart who prayed every day for his young friend. That man was the Apostle Paul.

The Apostle Paul, Timothy's father in ministry, encouraged the young minister to "stir up the gift of God, which is in thee" (2 Timothy 1:6).

Second Timothy 1:3-10 records:

> I thank God, whom I serve from my forefathers with pure conscience, that without ceasing I have remembrance of thee in my prayers night and day; greatly desiring to see thee, being mindful of thy tears, that I may be filled with joy; when I call to remembrance the unfeigned faith that is in thee, which dwelt first in thy grandmother Lois, and thy mother Eunice; and I am persuaded that in thee also. Wherefore I put thee in remembrance that thou stir up the gift of God, which is in thee by the putting on of my hands. For God hath not given us the spirit of fear; but of power, and of love, and of

a sound mind. Be not thou therefore ashamed of the testimony of our LORD, nor of me his prisoner: but be thou partaker of the afflictions of the gospel according to the power of God; who hath saved us, and called us with an holy calling, not according to our works, but according to his own purpose and grace, which was given us in Christ Jesus before the world began, but is now made manifest by the appearing of our Saviour Jesus Christ, who hath abolished death, and hath brought life and immortality to light through the gospel.

Much has been said and written about Paul laying hands on this young man and the ministry gift imparted to Timothy at that time. By studying the Scripture about Timothy, we can broaden our view to see the full range of life and power God deposited in him—and in us. Let's look at all those gifts Timothy needed to stir up, and examine what God had called him to do.

Questions for Reflection

1. What are some indicators in your life that you have been running on "empty"?

    _____

    _____

    _____

    _____

2. What has God called you to do that you may have placed on a shelf?

    _____

    _____

    _____

    _____

Take a moment to thank God right now for giving you the desire to stir up all He has placed in you!

Notes:

_____

_____

_____

_____

_____

_____

_____

_____

_____

_____

_____

_____

_____

_____

_____

_____

2

CHAPTER

STIR UP
REAL
FAITH

STIR UP
REAL
FAITH

"I call to remembrance *the unfeigned faith* that is in thee…" (2 Timothy 1:5).

The first thing Paul mentioned that Timothy had in him was *faith*. Paul called it "unfeigned" faith—not phony faith but the God kind of faith—the real thing from God.

Any real faith comes from God. Ephesians 2:8 says, "For by grace are ye saved through faith; and that not of yourselves: it is the gift of God." It's clear to me from Scripture, that the faith God gives us is the same faith by which He operates.

This raises a question with some people. I once had a man challenge me on this. He jumped all over me to make his point, saying, "God doesn't have faith."

"He doesn't?" I asked.

"No," he said. "He's the object of our faith. He doesn't have faith."

"Then where did I get the faith I have?" I responded. "If I didn't get it from God, I don't want it."

The man said, "God has faith to give, but He doesn't use faith."

Maybe the man was just too educated for his own good, or for me to understand, but I just couldn't figure that out. Besides that, he came too late. I was already using the faith God gave me!

I was using the mountain-moving faith Jesus told us to use in Mark 11:22-25 when He said, "Have faith in God," or "Have the God kind of faith." I was already living my life "by the faith of the Son of God, who loved me, and gave himself for me" (Galatians 2:20). The faith I had in me as a gift of God was the very same faith by which "the worlds were framed" (Hebrews 11:3).

Timothy's mother and grandmother lived by this gift of real faith, and Paul, convinced that same faith was in Timothy, encouraged him saying, "When I call to remembrance the unfeigned faith that is in thee, which dwelt first in thy grandmother Lois, and thy mother Eunice; and I am persuaded that in thee also"(2 Timothy 1:5). Paul was telling Timothy he was convinced the same genuine faith that was in Timothy's mother and grandmother was working in him also.

Apparently, Paul hadn't seen much of it, yet he was convinced all Timothy needed to do was stir up the faith he already had. He knew Timothy had the God kind of faith resident within him as a believer—the same kind of faith by which Jesus operated and which God gives every believer. As Timothy allowed that faith to come alive in him, it would link him with God's Anointing to do things in his daily life and ministry he could never do in his own strength. What the apostle was encouraging Timothy to do was to *stir up* that gift of faith present in him.

When you believe The WORD of God, you ignite a spark inside you that lights a fire you can't get any other way.

I remember, years ago, when we got our first butane grill with an igniter on it. On our previous grills, we would turn on the gas, throw in a match and hope for the best. But on this new one, I could just turn on the butane, push a button, and *whoom!,* it shot a spark across the gas vent, and we had an instant flame. The first day we had it, I turned it off and back on again, just to watch that igniter spark that fire into action.

That's what happens to your faith when you stir up the gift of God inside you. When you believe The WORD of God, add the confession of your mouth and praise from your heart, just like that gas grill, you ignite a spark inside you that lights a fire you can't get any other way. It's the unfeigned faith of God in you!

Questions for Reflection

1. Who in your life was or is an example of strong faith? What have you learned from that person?

_____

_____

_____

_____

2. Have you had times when you relied on faith in your own strength to accomplish what God has called you to do? What happened?

_____

_____

_____

_____

3. Describe a time in your life when your faith was sparked inside you!

_____

_____

_____

_____

Notes:

_____

_____

_____

_____

_____

_____

_____

_____

_____

_____

_____

_____

_____

_____

_____

_____

3

CHAPTER

STIR UP THE
POWER
OF GOD IN YOU

STIR UP THE POWER OF GOD IN YOU

"For God hath not given us the spirit of fear; but of power..." (2 Timothy 1:7).

Accompanying that genuine, God kind of faith in Timothy was a whole arsenal of spiritual resources. One of the first Paul mentions is *power*. Paul was encouraging Timothy, saying, "There's power in you, Timothy. Stir up the power."

I saw that power firsthand when I was a student at Oral Roberts University. I watched Oral Roberts use his faith like a mechanic uses a tool. He used it on purpose. He directed it. Though it stirred me, at first I didn't know that same power I watched him operate in to heal the sick and set captives free was available to me and already in me.

In fact, the first time I went with the Oral Roberts ministry team to a healing meeting, I nearly quit and went home. I was a student and a member of his aircraft flight crew. I had been born again for less than five years, and knew very little about the things of God—and even less about meetings like these. But, I was eager to learn how to minister in the power of God.

I was eager to learn how to minister in the power of God.

After we landed on my first ministry flight, I didn't have any other assignment, so I followed the team inside the huge auditorium. It turned out that meeting place was *filled* with sick people wanting to get prayed for. And they weren't just a little bit sick, either. The place was so full of disease and the smell so foul, it turned my stomach. Just walking into the place sent chills of fear up my spine. I didn't know what to do with it or how to handle it.

Understand now, these were people you just didn't see out on the streets in our society—especially in 1967. Just stumbling into the intensity of the enemy's devastation in that building, after living 30 years in unbelief, it didn't take me long to decide I was in the wrong place.

Just as quickly as I walked in, I turned on my heel and headed for a side door, talking to God under my breath. "Listen, I don't belong here," I told Him. "Nope, this isn't for me. I'm through with this. You can do what You want with that airplane. Oral Roberts or no Oral Roberts, I'm in the wrong place. I'm headed back to Tulsa. I don't care what I have to do to get there. Anything is better than this!"

I had never even prayed for anyone—never seen anyone prayed for, especially for anything that an aspirin couldn't fix. I had no idea what to do with what I was seeing and feeling. All I wanted to do was take the first bus out of there, and let them figure out how to get that airplane home.

After two steps outside the door, I started talking out loud to God: "I'm through, You understand that?"

Suddenly I froze. My feet wouldn't move. It was like my shoes were fastened to the sidewalk. Inside, I was still on the way to the bus station. Outside, I was stuck to the concrete. It was obvious who had stopped me.

"Let me loose!" I looked up and cried out to God. A war was raging within me. A fear like nothing I had ever experienced was driving me to run, yet a strange pull from God was drawing me back to what was going on inside the auditorium.

"Let me go," I insisted. "I don't have anything to give anyone in there. I don't have anything for those people."

Then God spoke to me. Whether human ears could have heard it, I don't know, but every cell in me heard His voice:

I know you don't have anything to give them, but I do. And that's why I baptized you in My Spirit.

When He finished speaking, my feet were freed, and I knew the choice was mine. I could go ahead and catch the bus back to Tulsa, or I could turn around and go back into that meeting. By that time, it was clear to me that my real choice was between spiritual life and spiritual death, and there was no doubt which one I wanted. Suddenly, I didn't want to get on that bus. I couldn't wait to get back in there. When I stepped back inside, I still didn't know what to do, and said to God, "What do I do now?"

I heard The LORD say, *Nothing. Just watch and pray and do what I tell you. Do what the men over you tell you to do, do what Brother Roberts tells you to do, and watch him.* That night, something stirred on the inside of me—

something that didn't want to run or back out anymore. It was a beginning for me. Until that night, I didn't know that healing faith was *in me*. I was ready to run, but God stopped me. He knew what was in me, and if I'd just stay, recognize the faith and power already resident within me and stir them up, miracles would happen!

Questions for Reflection

1. Describe a time you experienced the power of God in such strength it made you want to run away.

   _____

   _____

   _____

   _____

2. In what ways has the power of God worked mightily on your behalf?

   _____

   _____

   _____

   _____

3. What are some ways God's power has worked *through you* on behalf of others?

   _____

   _____

   _____

   _____

Notes:

_____

_____

_____

_____

_____

_____

_____

_____

_____

_____

_____

_____

_____

_____

_____

_____

CHAPTER

STIR UP THE
LOVE
OF GOD IN YOU

STIR UP THE LOVE
OF GOD IN YOU

"God hath not given us the spirit of fear; but of power, *and of love,* and of a sound mind" (2 Timothy 1:7).

Not only had God given Timothy the spirit of power, but He also had given him the spirit *of love.* Paul challenged him to understand that the God kind of love was in him—the unselfish, unconditional love of God.

In the same way, we must understand and stir up the love of God in us. Medical experts have some understanding of this in the natural realm. Many studies have shown that people need to receive expressions of love from others to live healthy, successful and emotionally stable lives. Humans need to hear, feel and see they are loved, valued and appreciated by other human beings.

Spouses, children, family, friends and all the people with whom we come in contact, need to experience our positive actions and words of kindness and compassion, rather than words of anger, frustration or disappointment. The same holds true for those with whom we spend time each day, whether in workplaces, educational settings or correctional facilities. We must develop the ability to convey in some way that God's love is there for them, too.

Stir up the love that's in you! Don't wait until you feel like it or have the time to do it. Love doesn't ask how you feel about it. God has placed His love in you so it's available all the time, ready to be released into any situation when needed. You only need to develop the ability to release that love.

Look again at 2 Timothy 1:7: "God hath not given us the spirit of fear...." If you are a born-again child of God, fear is *not* natural to you. The fountain of fear has been shut off in your heart. Now, you've got a fountain of faith inside you. If you don't develop that faith and stir it up, however, it'll lie dormant and your flesh will overcome it. In the same way, if you fail to develop God's love in you, it will lie unused while the fruit of wrong thinking and deception flood your mind.

God's love isn't limited to your feelings.
Choose by faith to love with the
God kind of love.

How do you develop God's love in you? Stir it up as an act of your faith instead of a response to your feelings. You may not feel like loving your husband, your wife, another family member, friend or co-worker. If you are incarcerated, you may not feel like loving that person assigned to the same prison block. Don't let that stop you. God's love isn't limited to your feelings. Choose by faith to love with the God kind of love, the same love that Romans 5:8 says loved *you* while you were yet a sinner!

In the Greek language, Jesus chose the word *agape* to describe the God kind of love. It means: "I love you because I promise to love you. I love you, not for what I can get out of you, but because I *choose* to love you. I love you regardless of you, and will continue to love you regardless of what you do or say. You are loved forever. I swear to it!"

This is the kind of love Jesus was praying about in John 17:26 when He said, "I have declared unto them thy name, and will declare it: that the love wherewith thou hast loved me may be in them, and I in them."

You can't do anything bad enough to make God turn from His promise of "I will never leave thee, nor forsake thee" (Hebrews 13:5). His is a love that can forgive the most heinous offender. And that same love is in you and me.

On death row in a Texas prison, Gloria and I ministered to and fellowshipped with a woman who had discovered that kind of love. She was sentenced to execution for the ax murders of her boyfriend and another woman. When she went through her trial, she showed no remorse. But in jail, she accepted Jesus as Savior and made Him The LORD of her life. That's when the remorse hit her and those deaths sorrowed her heart. She began reading The WORD, receiving God's forgiveness, and praying for the relatives and friends of her victims. She became so full of the love of God that every woman who came on death row on her cell block was born again and filled with the Spirit of God. What the system labeled "death row," those women renamed "life row."

In another prison, the minister—a man once on death row himself—had the men list the names of their victims on one side of a board, and on the other side, write the names of the officials who had caught them, the wardens, guards and whomever was over them in prison at that time. Once all the names were written before them, serious prayer began. The minister had them pray in the Name of Jesus and the power of the Holy Spirit for their victims, the families affected, and the prison staff. Their prayers became so powerful that on a couple of occasions when guards walked in the room in the middle of their prayer time, the power of God knocked the guards flat on their backs. Those inmates were stirring up the love of God planted in their reborn spirits!

Does it surprise you that men and women who have committed those kinds of crimes can pray that way? Remember 2 Corinthians 5:17 says, "If any man be in Christ, he is a new creature: old things are passed away; behold, all things are become new."

Men and women are capable of doing such serious things that tragically affect so many lives that it's extremely difficult to turn them around in this life. But as far as God is concerned, those same men and women can become born-again children of God. His love *can* change them.

The love it takes to make completely new creatures out of those prisoners is the same unconditional love it took to make a new creature out of you. That's the kind of powerful love God has deposited in your heart. Be aware of hurting people wherever you go, and look for opportunities to share that love in places you might not have considered before. Get beyond your front door. Allow God to help you step out of your comfort zone.

No matter where you happen to be, you'll find people hungry for the love of Christ through the gospel. Stir up the love of God that's within you. Stir it up...by faith!

Questions for Reflection

1. Who in your life has God given you to share His love with on a daily basis?

_____

_____

_____

_____

2. Describe a time when God's love rose in you and you saw someone through His eyes.

_____

_____

_____

_____

3. In what ways would God have you share His love with strangers?

_____

_____

_____

_____

Notes:

_____

_____

_____

_____

_____

_____

_____

_____

_____

_____

_____

_____

_____

_____

_____

_____

_____

_____

_____

5

CHAPTER

STIR UP
SOUND
THINKING

STIR UP
SOUND
THINKING

"God hath not given us the spirit of fear; but of power, and of love, *and of a sound mind*" (2 Timothy 1:7).

You won't stir up this kind of power and love by feeding your mind the wrong things. Paul reminded Timothy that God had given him not only the spirit of love and of power, but also of a *sound mind*. Do you want to shut the devil up? Do you want to silence those negative voices that keep rising up in your mind? Then, you'll have to stir up your thinking about the things of God!

God is not holding out on us. He's provided everything we need through Jesus Christ, the Anointed One and His Anointing. He's given us His WORD, His thoughts that are higher than our thoughts, and His ways that are higher than our ways. If you'll think about it, the only real problem any of us has is lack of knowledge of

God. He simply says, "My people are destroyed for lack of knowledge" (Hosea 4:6).

Proverbs 29:18 says that God's people also perish for lack of vision or a lack of insight into God and into their situations. Most people find themselves deeply involved in a problem before they ever look for vision or insight from God. They should have been praying and believing God before they ever got into the problem.

The things that distract believers from sound thinking based on God's WORD are often things that seem very important and even urgent. We see this vividly in Luke 10, where we read about two sisters who were hosting Jesus and His disciples.

One of the sisters, Mary, was sitting at Jesus' feet listening to Him teach, but Martha, the other sister, was bustling around in the kitchen cooking dinner for everyone.

Finally, Martha couldn't take it anymore. She came to Jesus and said, "LORD, don't You care that my sister has left me to do all the work myself? Tell her to help me!"

Jesus answered, "Martha, Martha, thou art careful and troubled about many things: But one thing is needful: and Mary hath chosen that good part, which shall not be taken away from her" (verses 41-42).

Mary chose to set everything else aside so she could hear The WORD. Martha allowed herself to be caught up in the circumstances surrounding her. She thought she was doing the right thing and had made a good choice, but Jesus said only one thing was *needful*. Being full of The WORD was more important than her service. Jesus was saying the primary thing she needed—the answer—was The WORD first. She should have chosen The WORD above all.

Remember, it is The WORD of God that made us free when we were born again. And it's The WORD that will *keep* us free as long as we feed on it continuously. The WORD of God is His wisdom for all our needs. It's what enables us to live without being bound to this world's system of death.

The devil is well aware of this and wants to convince us that we're really controlled by our minds. He wants to keep us from doing what The WORD says: "Casting down imaginations, and every high thing that exalteth itself against the knowledge of God, and bringing into captivity every thought to the obedience of Christ" (2 Corinthians 10:5).

According to this verse, we are to *take control of,* not to *be controlled by,* our minds.

Philippians 4:8-9 says:

> Finally, brethren, whatsoever things are true, whatsoever things are honest, whatsoever things are just, whatsoever things are pure, whatsoever things are lovely, whatsoever things are of good report; if there be any virtue, and if there be any praise, think on these things. Those things, which ye have both learned, and received, and heard, and seen in me, do: and the God of peace shall be with you.

We *can* take control of our own thought lives completely by speaking to and immediately casting down wrong thoughts, and choosing right thoughts to replace them. What are right thoughts? They are, according to this verse, things that are true, honest, just, pure, lovely and of good report. Jesus is all those things!

When we find ourselves worrying, if we'll shut down that worry immediately and think on Jesus, those thoughts will lose their power. Worry is nothing more than meditating on the lies of the devil. So don't do it. Meditate on Jesus, instead. Tell Satan, "I refuse to think on your junk! I choose to believe God's WORD. I'm going to think on Jesus and the promises in His WORD!"

Make the decisions that will put you over in the anointing and keep you there. Remind yourself you are the dwelling place of God's Spirit. Faith, love, joy, peace, temperance, long-suffering—all the fruit of the spirit are in you, ready to produce holiness, drive out all darkness and fear, and do everything God gave them to you to do. They're functioning in you in the same way your physical organs function inside your physical body. But just as the physical body must be fed physical food to become strong, the fruit of the spirit in you must be fed The WORD of God to become strong.

You are the dwelling place of God's Spirit. Faith, love, joy, peace, temperance, long-suffering—all the fruit of the spirit are in you.

Take a look at what you're spending most of your time listening to and watching. Is it filled with love, faith and sound thinking? You can choose to feed on God's wisdom or the world's wisdom. But what you put inside you will determine your future. Commit yourself to stay free by putting His WORD first place in your life and helping others to be made free, as well.

Stir up your faith. Stir up the power of God in you. Stir up the love of God in you. Stir up the sound mind that's already yours by feeding it with The WORD of God!

Questions for Reflection

1. When faced with a situation that tempts you to think like the world thinks, how do you refocus and think like God thinks?

_____

_____

_____

_____

2. What is your strategy to cast down imaginations and bring your thoughts captive to the obedience of Christ?

_____

_____

_____

_____

3. How do you regularly draw on the truths of Philippians 4:8-9 in your thought processes?

_____

_____

_____

_____

Notes:

6 ▲ CHAPTER

STIR UP
ETERNAL
LIFE

STIR UP
ETERNAL
LIFE

"Be thou partaker of the afflictions of the gospel according to the power of God" (2 Timothy 1:8).

Many believers can remember a time early in their Christian walk when they were so excited about their newfound faith in Jesus, they didn't mind grabbing everyone they saw and telling them, "Listen to what faith will do! Jesus is alive!" But after a while, they allowed the excitement to wane and were tempted to feel that maybe they had "graduated" from all that excitement stuff. Or, maybe because of opposition, they backed down from boldly sharing their testimony.

Boldly sharing your testimony is not something from which you "graduate," and it's often true that when you stir up your testimony and share it with others, it *can* bring opposition and misunderstanding. But, Paul was reminding Timothy not to back off when opposition came.

The devil's persecutions and attacks come to steal The WORD in the believer. When God saved you, and imparted eternal life to you, He gave you His armor to defeat all the attacks of the evil one. The helmet of salvation (Ephesians 6:17) is part of that armor. The life force of God—the law of the Spirit of life in Christ Jesus—is on the inside of you right now (Romans 8:2). God's own faith, hope, mind and way of doing things are in that life force. He, in all His fullness, has taken up residence in you (John 14:17). Everything He has and is, is within you. All you have to do is just spark it, or stir it up!

One of the best things that ever happened to me was when I learned to say continually, "Eternal life is in me. The life of God, the thing that makes God *God* is dwelling on the inside of me. God loves me as much as He loves Jesus!"

Too many times we limit the flow of God's life through us by majoring on what we can't do. Instead, major on who He is, His life inside you, and what you *can* do because He does live in you (Philippians 4:13). When you walk by faith, there may be times you will be misunderstood. But don't let that stop you!

That kind of misunderstanding happened to a friend of mine, a strong man of faith, who was questioned by a panel of preachers. They asked him:

"Do you mean to tell us you've got the power to heal?"

"Most assuredly yes!" he answered. Then, noticing their obvious shock and disbelief, he added, "Now, wait a minute before you throw me out of here. That electrical receptacle on the wall has power in it. It's not where the power originates, but it's in there. In the same way, the power of God is in me. The power to heal or save, or do anything else, in the Name of Jesus doesn't originate with me, but it's in me because He's in me."

Do you see what my friend was doing? He was testifying of The LORD, and stirring up what was inside him. He didn't back off because of the pressure from those other preachers or because it might not seem humble. The basis for what he said was not in anything he could do in his own strength, but in Christ, the Anointed One and in His Anointing (Philippians 4:13).

Just remember, when you testify to the power of the gospel and witness to others about the eternal life that's at work in you, you're not talking from the basis of your own ability and accomplishments. You're talking from the basis of what God's Anointing is accomplishing *through you,* who you are in Christ and who He is *in you!*

♦

When you testify, you're talking from
the basis of what God's Anointing is
accomplishing *through you.*

That's the basis on which Paul could emphatically say
he had "defrauded no man," (2 Corinthians 7:2), though
before he made Jesus his LORD, he had aggressively
persecuted the Church and been part of the stoning
of Stephen (Acts 22:20). The first time I read those
words, I genuinely thought Paul had to be a liar. I only
had to flip back a few pages in my Bible to see where
Paul certainly *had* defrauded men and women for their
belief in Christ and had them thrown into prison.

As I questioned Paul's claim, the Spirit of God spoke
up on the inside of me with a power that seemed it
could have knocked me over backward in my chair. He
said, *You watch who you call a liar! That man you're talking
about died on the road to Damascus. This is a new man.
This is a new creature in Christ Jesus. You've been going by
the wrong birthday. You're dealing with the birth of a man's
body. I deal with the birth of a man's spirit!*

That's good, isn't it? The revelation of eternal life and
being a new creature in Christ Jesus started growing on

the inside of me. I began to believe the love that God had for me and when I did, I found the scripture where Jesus said, "Father, show them that You love them as much as You do Me." That's the revelation the Apostle Paul grew in until he could say, "I am crucified with Christ: nevertheless I live; yet not I, but Christ liveth in me: and the life which I now live in the flesh I live by the faith of the Son of God, who loved me, and gave himself for me" (Galatians 2:20).

So, stir up the eternal life that's in *you!* As you go through the daily activities of life, say out loud,

"I have eternal life in me, now. I am forgiven and I forgive everyone who has hurt or come against me. That eternal life is illuminating my mind and my spirit. It's healing my body and delivering me from the onslaughts of darkness. The law of the Spirit of life in Christ Jesus has made me free from the law of sin and death. Eternal life is giving me the very wisdom of God Himself. I have the eternal life of God in me!"

Questions for Reflection

1. How often do you take the opportunity to tell others how eternal life is working in you?

_____

_____

_____

_____

2. When was a time you received opposition when sharing your testimony?

_____

_____

_____

_____

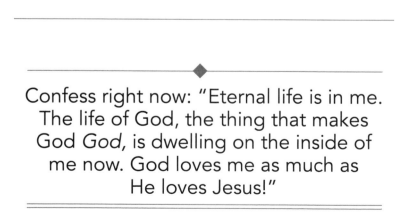

Confess right now: "Eternal life is in me. The life of God, the thing that makes God *God*, is dwelling on the inside of me now. God loves me as much as He loves Jesus!"

Notes:

_____

_____

_____

_____

_____

_____

_____

_____

_____

_____

_____

_____

_____

_____

_____

_____

_____

_____

_____

7

STIR UP THE
CALLING
OF GOD

STIR UP THE CALLING OF GOD

"Who hath saved us, and called us with an holy calling...according to his own purpose..." (2 Timothy 1:9).

Times of spiritual dryness can result from losing sight of the holy calling of God on your life. Paul reminded Timothy that the same God who "hath saved us" has also "called us with an holy calling...according to his own purpose and grace, which was given us in Christ Jesus."

One of the things you can do to stir up the gift within you is to go back to "the basics." You can return to the fundamentals of what God called you to do earlier in your walk with Him. If He called you to a healing ministry, go back to that and stir up that calling. Stir up that flow of God's supply and power for the things He has specifically called you to do. Stir up who you are in Christ Jesus. Say, "Praise God, I'm going back to my first love!"

That doesn't mean what you are doing now is wrong. But what it does mean is don't get distracted from the things God has called you to. He hasn't changed the call and purpose for your life: "For the gifts and calling of God are without repentance" (Romans 11:29).

So stir up the purpose of God inside your spirit. Cut off the outside distractions. Once you find out what God wants you to do, make a quality decision that nothing will keep you from doing it. Stir yourself up inside and out to accomplish what God has called you to do.

◆

Stir yourself up inside and out to accomplish what God has called you to do.

Over the years, another friend of mine got involved in so many different areas of ministry, he was about to fold up physically under the strain of it. Finally, The LORD spoke to him one night and said, *John, it's not My work that's nearly killed you. It's everything you've added to it.*

I've had to deal with that same thing in my own life. I've had to stop doing good things just because they needed doing. Instead, I've had to stick to what *I'm* called to do.

Maybe it's time for you to trim away the extra things you've added and get back to what God called you to do. Go back and stir up that original commission. It's holy. It's your personal calling!

Questions for Reflection

1. When was the last time you sensed spiritual dryness?

_____

_____

_____

_____

2. What distractions are impeding your fulfilling God's call on your life?

_____

_____

_____

3. How can you integrate your calling from God into your daily life?

_____

_____

_____

_____

Notes:

_____

_____

_____

_____

_____

_____

_____

_____

_____

_____

_____

_____

_____

_____

_____

_____

_____

_____

CHAPTER

8

STIR UP THE
CARE
OF GOD FOR YOU

STIR UP THE CARE
OF GOD FOR YOU

"...Without ceasing I have remembrance of thee in my prayers night and day...being mindful of thy tears" (2 Timothy 1:3-4).

Nothing can cause a believer to starve his spirit and stir up the devil more quickly than to become focused on his own hurts, persecutions and cares, and to begin thinking God has abandoned him.

Look back at 2 Timothy 1:2-4 at how Paul began his letter to Timothy:

> To Timothy, my dearly beloved son.... I thank God, whom I serve from my forefathers with pure conscience, that without ceasing I have remembrance of thee in my prayers night and day; greatly desiring to see thee, being mindful

of thy tears, that I may be filled with joy.

These aren't the words of a casual acquaintance. These are words from a spiritual father, a man filled with the Spirit of Christ. He was easily touched with the feelings of Timothy's infirmities. Day and night without ceasing, Paul writes, he remembers Timothy in prayer, mindful of the young minister's tears—mindful of his hurts and the way in which he was wounded.

But notice, once he had said that, Paul didn't talk anymore about those hurts and tears. Apparently, the answer to the needs of this young minister Paul cared about so deeply was not to be found in focusing on Timothy's situation. The answer was in getting Timothy's attention back on what God had deposited in his life and called him to do. Essentially, Paul was saying: "I am mindful of your tears, but I am convinced that you have the same kind of real, God-ordained faith in you that your mother had in her."

I want you to meditate on these next few sentences with your mind locked on to The WORD of God and your heart grounded in the confidence of your heavenly Father's deep care for you: Your hurts and your tears— your wounds, pains, sicknesses, diseases, irritations, loneliness, burnout, weariness and persecutions—are very, very important to Jesus. God cares about you. Other members of the Body of Christ care about you. What you should be focused on is not those trials and tears, but what your brothers and sisters in Christ are going through and what God has called *you* to do.

What you should be focused on is not those trials and tears, but what God has called you to do.

For me to stop reacting to my personal pains and problems, I had to make a firm, quality, Rock-founded, blood-washed decision. I decided I was through asking Kenneth Copeland how he feels. Now, I *tell* Kenneth Copeland how he feels. I don't ask my body what it thinks. If I did, it'd tell me it's sick, tired, worn-out and pitiful. I don't ask other believers who might comment based on what they see. Instead, I ask The WORD, and it's the same every time. It says I'm healed. It says, "If there be any virtue, and if there be any praise, think on these things" (Philippians 4:8).

How other people respond to my needs should have no effect on what I think about myself or on how I respond to them. I had to learn that in my relationship with my wife.

One day, early in our ministry, I became very irritated with Gloria because she hadn't made me eggs for breakfast. It was right after God had called Gloria to preach, and she was working on a sermon. I got mad at God for calling her to preach!

"Ah, she doesn't care anyway," I mouthed off under my breath as I walked out of the room. The stupidity coming out of my mouth did not go unnoticed by The LORD.

What difference does that make? He asked.

"What?"

You said she doesn't care, He said.

"That's what I said."

What difference does that make? He said again. *It's none of your business whether she cares or not.*

I wasn't used to hearing talk like that. Maybe you're like me and grew up hearing people say, "Oh, nobody cares about me. That's the reason I am like I am. My parents didn't care. My schoolteachers didn't care. Nobody cares about me. Nobody ever gave me anything."

But that day, The LORD put an end to those words coming out of my mouth. *It's none of your business whether anyone cares about you or not,* He said. *That's not your concern. It's your business whether you care about her or not. Now, you tend to that.*

My business is to know that God Almighty cares for me. I'm to live my life serving the One who cares for me first and died for me. I'm to stir up the love of God in me, the care of God in me and the faith of God in me. That realization absolutely turned my life right-side up.

It's not any of my business what you think about me. It's not even my business if you care about me. My job is to know that *Almighty God* cares for me and to stir up the love He's put in me for you. My business is caring about you!

Questions for Reflection

1. When was a time when you were so focused on your challenges that you felt God had abandoned you?

_____

_____

_____

_____

2. How did you free yourself from those thoughts of abandonment?

_____

_____

_____

_____

3. Who has God placed in your life to care for you? And who has He placed in your life to receive *your* care?

_____

_____

_____

_____

4. How do you daily allow The LORD to help you to cast all your cares (both received and given) onto Him?

_____

_____

_____

_____

Notes:

9

CHAPTER

STIR UP THE JOY

STIR UP THE JOY

"Now the God of hope fill you with all joy and peace in believing, that ye may abound in hope, through the power of the Holy Ghost" (Romans 15:13).

Although Paul didn't mention it in his exhortation to Timothy, his letters are filled with references to another fruit of the spirit we need to stir up if we're to ride on the high places of the earth with God (Isaiah 58:14). We need to stir up the *joy* that's within us.

Years ago, I decided to walk by The WORD of God. Whatever The WORD says I am, that's what I'm saying, too. I told God as far as I was concerned, His WORD was final, and I'd confess it—speak it out loud—the rest of my life, no matter what. That turned out to be one of the most important decisions I ever made.

Not too long after that, I made another life-changing decision that no matter what happened, whether I felt like it or not, I'd walk in God's love toward others because the Bible clearly says "faith worketh by love" (Galatians 5:6). According to The WORD of God, it won't work any other way.

Those two important decisions—to operate by faith in The WORD of God and to walk in love—have forever changed the course of my life and ministry.

God pointed out to me that I have no right to walk by faith and love and just ignore joy and leave it lying there. After all, joy is just as much a part of the fruit of the spirit as love and faith. In fact, the fruit of joy is so powerful that Nehemiah 8:10 says, "The joy of The LORD is your strength"!

Joy is just as much a part of the fruit of the spirit as love and faith.

To keep joy stirred up in me, there were certain things I had to do. For instance, a number of years ago I promised God I'd never read anything about myself in print—good or bad, and ordered my staff to never bring me anything in print about me. I committed that

I would set myself to hear from God only on how I was doing in my walk with Him.

I was also being very stringent with myself because of a challenge I had dealt with and overcome, through the years, with anger. Back in the old days, I had a hair-trigger temper. If it looked like there might be any argument at all, I'd hit you before it started, hoping we could then discuss it on my terms. It was best for me to stop concerning myself with what other people said.

You may not have to be that stringent in this area of your own life, but you must do whatever it takes to stay in joy. The fact is, if you don't stir up the joy of The LORD within you, you'll begin having trouble walking in faith and love. You'll be too weak to hang on to them. Oh, you may loudly declare, "I'm standing on The WORD. I'm walking by faith." But, if you're not rejoicing, I can guarantee you'll get tired.

You can't leave joy out of this stirring-up process. Make the strong commitment to God that whatever comes, you're walking in joy. No matter what the devil does or what anyone says to you or about you, you're going to rejoice!

Questions for Reflection

1. How do you most often express your joy in The LORD?

_____

_____

_____

_____

2. What situations in your life most often try to steal your joy?

_____

_____

_____

_____

3. In what ways have you experienced "the joy of The LORD" being your strength?

_____

_____

_____

_____

Notes:

▲ CHAPTER

10

FROM A DRY GOURD TO A WELLSPRING OF LIFE

FROM A DRY GOURD TO A
WELLSPRING
OF LIFE

In his care for and ministry to Timothy, Paul made one thing very clear to the young man: The decision to stir yourself up is your *choice*, and it must be based on faith, not feelings.

I certainly didn't feel like rejoicing during those early days of daily television. In fact, in the middle of my emptiness and constant concern about how we would do it, Gloria said to me, "I don't understand what you're so upset about."

"Don't you understand?" I replied. "We're going broke. We're going down the tubes."

"Well, I don't understand what you're so upset about," she said again. "It's your choice. You can believe God or get in that frenzy. It all takes the same amount of time."

Of course, that aggravated me. What do you do with someone like that? God had already told me Gloria was to me what tempering is to steel. Steel is brittle until you temper it. She's the tempering process to me—the stability behind The WORD of God, and so often a role model to me of how I ought to act by faith. So, I received what she said!

Shortly after that, my friend Jerry Savelle was preaching in Little Rock, Arkansas, in celebration of his and Carolyn's many years in ministry. That night, Jerry began by reading the same words from 2 Timothy I've shared with you: "Being mindful of thy tears.... I put thee in remembrance that thou stir up the gift of God, which is in thee" (2 Timothy 1:4, 6).

I was startled when I heard that. Apparently, Timothy had been discouraged just like me. Apparently, he'd felt inadequate to the task God had given him. But Paul addressed the problem with a clear command: "Stir up the gift inside you." In other words, *You stir yourself up!"*

I saw it in a flash. The Spirit of God is in me already. Jesus is in me. I'm in Him, and all I need is in Him. Every resource I'll ever need to do what God has called me to do is inside me. All I need is to stir up those resources!

I said right out loud, "In the Name of Jesus, I stir myself up, by faith! I stir up the gift that's within me. In Jesus' Name, I'm stirred up!"

I didn't feel a bit different. I didn't suddenly want to run home and start taping television broadcasts. In fact, I felt as weary as I had before. If I'd asked my body, "Are you stirred up?" it would have said, "Dear me, no. I need another 30 days of sleep!" But I didn't ask my body.

I turned to Gloria and said, "Gloria, I'm stirred up!" She smiled and agreed with me. She knew exactly what I was doing. It didn't matter if my eyes were bloodshot and my face was pale—she agreed with my confession of faith.

Something's Happening!

That night, to everyone with whom I shook hands, I declared, "Man, I'm stirred up. I am stirred up, brother. Whoa, I am stirred up!" I said it to everyone I saw. I said it to God. I even sat down and wrote it in a letter to my Partners.

You know what? It was only a few days until I suddenly noticed, *I AM stirred up! Something real has happened here.* Had that "something" been missing before? No! It was in me all along. But when I spoke, it started stirring until it began to affect my feelings.

◆

Everything you need is already in you. Jesus put it there.

That's how spiritual things always work. Feelings follow faith. Feelings weren't designed to lead. They were designed to follow. Everything you need is already in you. Jesus put it there. Everything you'll ever need to accomplish what God has called you to do has already been placed inside you by God Almighty.

Stir Up the Anointing That's in You

By His Anointing in you, on you and through you, God has empowered you to overflow with His life. Miracles, healings, acts of power, revelations and salvations are taking place everywhere, on every hand. Look for them everywhere you go. Most of all, look for them inside you. They will come *out of you* by the power of the Holy Spirit who lives *in you.*

One definition of *anointing* is "God on flesh, doing those things that flesh can't do." The anointing is His presence and power, together with a human being's flesh, carrying out God's plan of redemption in the earth.

This is spelled out clearly in 2 Corinthians 4:7: "But we have this treasure in earthen vessels, that the excellency of the power may be of God, and not of us." Christ (the Anointed One and His Anointing; the Holy Spirit poured on for service) in us, is our hope of glory (Colossians 1:27). Jesus has provided the same presence of God the Father Himself for us in our earthly ministries that He had in His earthly ministry. The more you get involved in what God is doing, the more He is involved in what you're doing. His Anointing will come alive in you, on you and through you.

Expect the anointing. Spark that life on the inside of you with The WORD of God. Let it rise up within you as you saturate yourself with His promises and provisions. Continue in His WORD and in fellowship with Him until His life not only rises up inside you, but overflows from you so that out of your belly flow rivers of living water—anointing—to go about doing good, bringing salvation and deliverance to everyone around you!

We've seen significant displays of faith in the Body

of Christ in recent years. Jesus is on the move. The glory is here! We'll be seeing more of His glory and power than we've ever seen before. The Spirit of God is moving in enormous power, and it's time we move with Him!

Let the living force of God, the living healing of God, the living hope of God, the living faith of God, the living presence of God rise up on the inside of you. Let them not only take care of every situation you face, but spill over in demonstration to all men that His glory on earth is working through those who walk in covenant with Him.

Let the living force of God rise up on the inside of you.

Don't wait until you "feel" like you can do it. Don't wait until you feel anything! Start stirring yourself up, and watch what happens.

Say this out loud with me, now:

◆

"In the Name of Jesus, I stir up the gift
that's within me by faith. I'm not waiting
until I feel something. I will begin feeling
it because I'm stirring it up. I'm stirring
up my faith. I'm stirring up the love of
God that's in me. I'm stirring up the
forgiveness that's in me. I'm stirring up
the power and the glory of God in me.
In the Name of Jesus, I'm stirring up
everyone around me. I'm stirring up my
church. I'm stirring up the devil, and
running him out of my affairs! I'm stirring
myself up in the Spirit of the living God!
I AM stirred up!"

Now quit waiting to *feel* like you can do it, and get
out there! Once you do, you'll discover that the power
you've been waiting for has been right there inside you
all the time...waiting for you. You have a job to do, and
you have everything you need to do it. STIR IT UP!

Questions for Reflection

1. Write about a story from your own life when you went from being a dry gourd to being a vessel of the anointing.

   _____

   _____

   _____

   _____

2. How can you allow the presence, power and love of the living God to flow from your life into the lives of people He brings your way?

   _____

   _____

   _____

   _____

   ───────────────◆───────────────

   If you did not pray the prayer on page 121 out loud, do it now!

Notes:

Keep yourself *stirred* up!

KCM Partners are invited to visit:

BELIEVERS' ACADEMY

···KCM.ORG/STIRYOURSELFUP·····

for a **FREE** 10-video teaching series on
how to Stop Spiritual Drought.

Prayer for Salvation and Baptism in the Holy Spirit

Heavenly Father, I come to You in the Name of Jesus. Your Word says, "Whosoever shall call on the name of the Lord shall be saved" (Acts 2:21). I am calling on You. I pray and ask Jesus to come into my heart and be Lord over my life according to Romans 10:9-10: "If thou shalt confess with thy mouth the Lord Jesus, and shalt believe in thine heart that God hath raised him from the dead, thou shalt be saved. For with the heart man believeth unto righteousness; and with the mouth confession is made unto salvation." I do that now. I confess that Jesus is Lord, and I believe in my heart that God raised Him from the dead.

I am now reborn! I am a Christian—a child of Almighty God! I am saved! You also said in Your Word, "If ye then, being evil, know how to give good gifts unto your children: HOW MUCH MORE shall your heavenly Father give the Holy Spirit to them that ask him?" (Luke 11:13). I'm also asking You to fill me with the Holy Spirit. Holy Spirit, rise up within me as I praise God. I fully expect to speak with other tongues as You give me the utterance (Acts 2:4). In Jesus' Name. Amen!

Begin to praise God for filling you with the Holy Spirit. Speak those words and syllables you receive—not in your own language, but the language given to you by the Holy Spirit. You have to use your own voice. God will not force you to speak. Don't be concerned with how it sounds. It is a heavenly language!

Continue with the blessing God has given you and pray in the spirit every day.

You are a born-again, Spirit-filled believer. You'll never be the same!

Find a good church that boldly preaches God's Word and obeys it. Become part of a church family who will love and care for you as you love and care for them.

We need to be connected to each other. It increases our strength in God. It's God's plan for us.

Make it a habit to watch the *Believer's Voice of Victory* television broadcast and become a doer of the Word, who is blessed in his doing (James 1:22-25).

About the Author

Kenneth Copeland is co-founder and president of Kenneth Copeland Ministries in Fort Worth, Texas, and best-selling author of books that include *How to Discipline Your Flesh* and *Honor—Walking in Honesty, Truth and Integrity*.

Since 1967, Kenneth has been a minister of the gospel of Christ and teacher of God's Word. He is also the artist on award-winning albums such as his Grammy-nominated *Only the Redeemed, In His Presence, He Is Jehovah, Just a Closer Walk* and *Big Band Gospel*. He also co-stars as the character Wichita Slim in the children's adventure videos *The Gunslinger, Covenant Rider* and the movie *The Treasure of Eagle Mountain,* and as Daniel Lyon in the Commander Kellie and the Superkids$_{TM}$ videos *Armor of Light* and *Judgment: The Trial of Commander Kellie*. Kenneth also co-stars as a Hispanic godfather in the 2009 movie *The Rally*.

With the help of offices and staff in the United States, Canada, England, Australia, South Africa, Ukraine and Singapore, Kenneth is fulfilling his vision to boldly preach the uncompromised Word of God from the top of this world, to the bottom, and all the way around. His ministry reaches millions of people worldwide through daily and Sunday TV broadcasts, magazines, teaching audios and videos, conventions and campaigns, and the World Wide Web.

Learn more about Kenneth Copeland Ministries by visiting our website at **kcm.org**

When The LORD first spoke to Kenneth and Gloria Copeland about starting the *Believer's Voice of Victory* magazine...

He said: *This is your seed. Give it to everyone who ever responds to your ministry, and don't ever allow anyone to pay for a subscription!*

For more than 40 years, it has been the joy of Kenneth Copeland Ministries to bring the good news to believers. Readers enjoy teaching from ministers who write from lives of living contact with God, and testimonies from believers experiencing victory through God's Word in their everyday lives.

Today, the *BVOV* magazine is mailed monthly, bringing encouragement and blessing to believers around the world. Many even use it as a ministry tool, passing it on to others who desire to know Jesus and grow in their faith!

Request your FREE subscription to the *Believer's Voice of Victory* magazine today!

Go to **freevictory.com** to subscribe online, or call us at **1-800-600-7395** (U.S. only) or **+1-817-852-6000**.

We're Here for You!®

Your growth in God's WORD and victory in Jesus are at the very center of our hearts. In every way God has equipped us, we will help you deal with the issues facing you, so you can be the **victorious overcomer** He has planned for you to be.

The mission of Kenneth Copeland Ministries is about all of us growing and going together. Our prayer is that you will take full advantage of all The LORD has given us to share with you.

Wherever you are in the world, you can watch the *Believer's Voice of Victory* broadcast on television (check your local listings), the Internet at kcm.org or on our digital Roku channel.

Our website, **kcm.org,** gives you access to every resource we've developed for your victory. And, you can find contact information for our international offices in Africa, Asia, Australia, Canada, Europe, Ukraine and our headquarters in the United States.

Each office is staffed with devoted men and women, ready to serve and pray with you. You can contact the worldwide office nearest you for assistance, and you can call us for prayer at our U.S. number, +1-817-852-6000, 24 hours every day!

We encourage you to connect with us often and let us be part of your everyday walk of faith!

Jesus Is LORD!

Kenneth & Gloria Copeland

Kenneth and Gloria Copeland